The Secret to a Happy Family

A Successful Family Resource Guide

Dr. Creflo A. Dollar and Taffi L. Dollar

Other Resource Guides in *The Successful Family* Series

Before the Ring
Marriage Enhancement
Family Planning and Children
Making a Go of It
Life on the Edge

The Secret to a Happy Family: Resource Guide
ISBN 1-59089-705-6
Copyright © 2002 by Dr. Creflo A. Dollar and Taffi L. Dollar

Published by:
Creflo Dollar Ministries
P.O. Box 490124
College Park, GA 30349

CONTENTS

HOW TO USE THIS RESOURCE GUIDE

S trong individuals make strong families. That is why this resource guide is a vital element in *The Successful Family* series. When used in conjunction with *Part IV: The Secret to a Happy Family*, of *The Successful Family* reference book, this guide becomes a dynamic tool that will assist you in achieving the success you desire in your relationships. It is a good idea to read and sign the commitment certificate in this guide before beginning your journey to a successful family.

There is no right or wrong way to use this guide. You may complete the exercises alone, with a partner or in a group. However, be sure to allow enough time to review the relevant chapters and complete the corresponding exercises. Don't give up if an exercise seems challenging. Press your way through, and ask someone for help, if necessary. Remember, your goal is to see what areas of your life need to be changed, and then make the appropriate adjustment with the Word of God.

Follow these steps to prepare for each exercise:

- Pray for wisdom
- Read the corresponding chapter(s) in part four of *The Successful Family*
- Complete the exercise(s)

- Apply what you learn to your life

For every problem there is a solution. You can make the most of your family life and become a solution-oriented person by studying the biblical principles in each exercise. And don't forget to enjoy the journey to successful, vibrant relationships!

MY COMMITMENT

If you are fed up with constant turmoil with your spouse and children and are serious about seeing change take place in your life, read the following statements and then sign your name at the bottom of this page. Make time in your daily schedule to give voice to your commitment to change so that you can remain focused.

- I will read *Part IV: The Secret to a Happy Family,* of *The Successful Family* and complete the corresponding exercises. If this is a group session, and I must miss a meeting, I will make up all missed assignments.
- I will designate a specific time frame daily in which to study the information and complete the exercises.
- If this is a group, I will be on time for each session. I realize that my tardiness is a distraction to others and causes me to miss out on valuable information.
- I will share my answers with a trusted friend and/or participate in group discussions.
- I will be honest with myself and/or other group members.
- I commit to love myself enough to successfully complete this session no matter how difficult or challenging the exercises seem.

- I will apply what I learn and periodically gauge my growth.

- I commit to confidentiality and will not discuss the personal affairs of others outside of the group.

_____   _____

        Signature   Date

Exercise One:

THE KEY TO CHANGE

In order for a family to be successful, everyone must be willing to change. Change, however, doesn't always come easy. Permanent change *cannot* occur unless family members are willing to "turn over a new leaf" and transform their thinking. Whether you realize it or not, the negative, ungodly thoughts you dwell on today will eventually become your future actions. By simply changing the way you think, you will change your behavior. Likewise, the more you meditate on, or think about, specific scriptures and apply them to your life, the more those biblical principles will transform you from the inside out. Unless the Word of God is your foundation, any changes you attempt to make will not last.

Just as colleges have introductory classes that must be taken before students can proceed to more advanced levels in their field, so you must know the basic truths regarding Christianity, salvation and mind renewal. Using chapter 24, *The Master Key*, as a guide, read each statement below and fill in the blanks with the correct responses.

1.   Every person is divided into three parts: _____, _____and _____.

2. You _____ a spirit. You _____ a soul. You _____ a body.

3. Your body eventually turns to _____; however, your _____ lives on.

4. If you have accepted Jesus Christ as your Lord and Savior, you will go to _____ when you die.

5. If you have not, you will spend eternity in _____.

6. Your soul consists of your _____, _____ and _____.

7. The body houses your _____ and your _____.

8. Before you became born again, your spirit was _____, or alienated from God by sin.

9. _____ is simply a state of being that entered the world when Adam disobeyed God.

10. After giving, or surrendering your life to Christ, your spirit is_____ and given _____ This is where we get the term, _____ _____.

11. Although the condition of your _____ changes automatically when you accept Jesus, your _____ and _____ do not.

12. You must make the effort to _____ or _____, your
    _____ so that your _____ _____ with the Word of
    God.

13. Only then will your _____, _____, _____
    and_____begin to line up with the _____ of your_____.

Exercise Two:

IDENTIFYING STRONGHOLDS

Often the ability or willingness to change is hindered by the presence of strongholds. A stronghold is a negative thought pattern that has developed through the words you hear and speak, suggestions you entertain and mental images you create. These thoughts cause you to react automatically to certain stimuli.

Take a moment to review the words listed below and their definitions. They represent several of the most common strongholds in a person's life. How do you find yourself reacting to each one? Write down those areas of your life where you believe a stronghold has developed, and how you plan to combat it. Remember, if you find yourself defending or justifying certain thoughts, opinions or actions, realize that a stronghold has taken up residence in your mind.

1. **Unbelief:** *You have trouble believing that the Word of God works.*

List the areas in your life where you struggle with this:_____

_____

_____

_____

2. **Pride:** *You find it difficult or impossible to admit your mistakes. You also refuse to comply with biblical principles and guidelines and rebel against authority.*

List areas in your life where you struggle with this:_____

_____

_____

_____

3. **Unforgiveness:** *You carry old hurts and have allowed bitterness and resentment to take root in your heart.*

List areas in your life where you struggle with this:_____

_____

_____

_____

4. **Lust:** *You struggle with, or cave in to, strong appetites. These can include sex, food, money, knowledge or power.*

List areas in your life where you struggle with this:_____

_____

_____

_____

_____

5. **Cold Love:** *You lack compassion, warmth and a tender heart.*

List areas in your life where you struggle with this:_____

_____

_____

_____

6. **Fear:** *You have a fear of failure, the unknown or present circumstances, or suffer from phobias.*

List areas in your life where you struggle with this:_____

_____

_____

_____

Congratulations! You have now uncovered what the enemy has kept hidden from you. Now look up scriptures that pertain to your situation. Use a concordance if necessary. Meditate on those scriptures until you are absolutely convinced they are true. Then confess, or speak them, aloud to combat those negative thoughts (2 Corinthians 10:5). Realize that it took more than one day for a stronghold to develop, and it may take more than one day to break free of it.

The strongest person doesn't always win life's battles. However, the determined person who believes that he or she will win always does. If you are experiencing inner conflict, rejoice! That confirms that you're at war with your old nature. Remember, victory is near: "*...in all these things we are more than conquerors through him that loved us*" (Romans 8:37)!

FROM CATERPILLAR TO BUTTERFLY

Here are 12 steps to assist you in reaching your goal of permanent change in your life. Under each step, write down how you will implement it. Before you begin, pray this prayer aloud: *"God, I want to change. I believe that the more I study and apply Your principles to my life, the more I will be transformed from the inside out. My relationships with my family are better than ever because I am eliminating old thought patterns and replacing them with new ones. Help me to continue on the path to self-improvement. In Jesus name, Amen."*

1. **Make a decision.**

What made you decide enough was enough? _____

_____

_____

_____

2. **Turn your will completely over to God.**

How will you submit?_____

_____

_____

_____

3. **Possess a strong desire to change.**

How will you watch your influences and focus on positive godly things?

_____

_____

_____

_____

4. **Deepen your knowledge base.**

In what ways are you committed to knowing more about God? _____

_____

_____

_____

5. **Look into the Word as a mirror for change.**

How do you plan to allow God's Word to serve as your spiritual mirror, revealing what needs to be changed? _____

_____

_____

_____

6. **Diligently apply the truths you've learned.**

How will you make sure that you don't forget to apply what you've learned?_____

_____

_____

_____

7.   **Guard the entrances to your heart.**

How committed are you to protect what your see, hear and say? _____

_____

_____

_____

8.   **Defend your mind against negative thoughts.**

How have you committed to taking every thought captive and bringing it under submission to God's Word? _____

_____

_____

_____

9.   **Be selective of what you expose yourself to.**

Are you committed to watching where you go and with whom you hang around? How?_____

_____

_____

_____

10.   **Disassociate from the past.**

How have you determined to press on and forget the past? _____

_____

_____

_____

11.   **Be open to correction and remain teachable.**

How will you guard against making excuses or justifying your behavior?

_____

_____

_____

_____

12.   Depend on God and others for support.

How have you determined to open your life to others in order to build a solid support base?_____
_____
_____
_____

Exercise Four:

TAMING THE TIGER

Have you ever heard the saying, "You are what you eat?" The same thing applies to your mind: you are what you think. Proverbs 23:7 says, *"For as [a man] thinketh in his heart, so is he."*

Take a moment to reflect on your thought life. What things do you dwell on the most? List them here:

1. _____   4. _____

2. _____   5. _____

3. _____   6. _____

Are your thoughts full of fear, insecurity, lust, spite or anger? Is this indicative of *who* you really are? Is there a problem area that needs adjustment? If so:

- Search the Bible for scriptures that pertain to your particular situation.

- Write the scriptures down.

- Post them in places where you will be able to reach them easily, including your car and wallet.

- When your mind begins to drift toward those thoughts, recite the scriptures aloud.

Do this every time you feel your mind drifting into "forbidden teritory." Before you know it, you will be free from those persistent, negative thoughts because you will have replaced them with God's Word!

Exercise Five:

BIBLE JEOPARDY

Have you ever watched the game show *Jeopardy?* The host of the show, Alex Trebek, reads an answer and the contestants have to respond to it by stating the question. In this exercise, you'll read a variety of "answers" that are nothing more than lies from the devil. As the contestant, you must write God's truth and the scripture that is the foundation for that truth.

1. *"You've got cancer. You're going to die."*

Truth:_____

_____

2. *"Your child is going to be shot. He'll die."*

Truth:_____

_____

3. *You remember what happened last time when it was dark."*

Truth:_____

_____

4. "No one will ever love you."

Truth:_____

_____

5. "Your plane is going to crash."

Truth:_____

_____

6. "You are a total failure. Do yourself a favor and just end it all."

Truth:_____

_____

Through the truth of God's Word, you are more than a conqueror!

Exercise Six:

SALVATION BASICS

Read each statement below and determine whether it is true (T) or false (F). When you are finished, compare your answers with the answer key at the back of this guide.

1. Before you became born again, your viewpoints   T   F
    were most often shaped by society, personal
    experience or the advice of others.

2. Becoming a born-again Christian is not the end   T   F
    of the process for building a successful family
    and life for yourself.

3. If an individual fails to overcome temptation,   T   F
    it means he is not a "genuine" Christian.

4. Your born-again status guarantees you eternal   T   F
    life in heaven, but no necessarily heaven on earth.

5. A stronghold is a negative thought pattern   T   F
    that has developed through the words you hear
    and speak, suggestions you entertain and mental
    images you create.

6. When you begin to align your thoughts with   T   F
   God's thoughts, you will experience a
   season of inner conflict.

7. Transforming your mind only takes a few short years.   T   F

Exercise Seven:

THE NAME GAME

Test your knowledge of the Bible by completing this exercise. Read the clues below and fill in the blanks on the next page with the correct answers. When you are finished, compare your responses with the answer key at the back of this guide.

1. King Solomon's rebellious official
2. Nickname of the singing Levite
3. Old Testament instruments
4. Paul's missionary partner
5. Celebrated doctor of the Jewish law who taught Paul
6. Found in a basket
7. A man after God's heart
8. New name of the man blinded by light
9. Female deliverer of Jews
10. City where Dorcas lived
11. Second son of Zilpah, Leah's maidservant
12. Also known as "the dreamer"
13. Physician and Paul's travelling companion
14. Told Hezekiah to put his house in order
15. Said, "Can two walk together, unless they be agreed?"
16. Peter used this to catch fish
17. Classy term for pottery
18. Appointed men to sing and praise God before battle
19. Was thrown into a den of lions
20. Twin son of Tamar
21. Wouldn't go to battle without Deborah
22. A whirlwind took him to heaven.
23. Had a message for the Edomites
24. Tentmaker and husband of Aquila
25. Mother of Solomon
26. Second son of Noah

28

27. Translated disciple

28. Denied Jesus three times

29. Plant that gave Jonah shade

30. Raised from the dead

31. Last book of Old Testament

32. Paul and Silas were here during an earthquake

33. Book before Revelation

34. Married Ruth

35. Godly king over Judah before Babylonian exile

36. Bathsheba's first husband

37. One of two who wanted to "take" the land

38. First mom

39. Today it's a story, then it was a measurement

40. He became profitable to Paul after they made up

41. First-born son of Abraham's brother

42. This king's feet became diseased in his old age in his old age

1. _____
2. _____
3. _____
4. _____
5. _____
6. _____
7. _____
8. _____
9. _____
10. _____
11. _____
12. _____
13. _____
14. _____
15. _____
16. _____
17. _____
18. _____
19. _____
20. _____
21. _____

22. _____
23. _____
24. _____
25. _____
26. _____
27. _____
28. _____
29. _____
30. _____
31. _____
32. _____
33. _____
34. _____
35. _____
36. _____
37. _____
38. _____
39. _____
40. _____
41. _____
42. _____

JOSEPH'S SECRET EGYPTIAN CODE

See if you can locate the secret Egyptian number code. Each clue will help to eliminate one or more numbers. Place an X on each number that you eliminate. You can use this game over and over with your family. Simply think of different questions each time to change the code. It's great learning fun for the children – and the family! Have fun!

This number is odd.

The digits of this number can be added together to make a total that is greater than 10.

This number does not have an 8 in the tens place.

When the smaller digit of this number is subtracted from the larger digit, the answer is 7.

The first digit of this number is smaller than the second digit.

What is the secret Egyptian number code?_____

1	2	3	4	5	6	7	8	9	10
11	12	13	14	15	16	17	18	19	20
21	22	23	24	25	26	27	28	29	30
31	32	33	34	35	36	37	38	39	40
41	42	43	44	45	46	47	48	49	50
51	52	53	54	55	56	57	58	59	60
61	62	63	64	65	66	67	68	69	70
71	72	73	74	75	76	77	78	79	80
81	82	83	84	85	86	87	88	89	90
91	92	93	94	95	96	97	98	99	100

Exercise Nine:

BIBLE TRIVIA

Have some family fun with these Bible Trivia questions. Allow the winner to choose the next game or meal, or come up with his or her own trivia questions for the entire family!

1. Who was the son of Saul who risked his life to help David?
2. According to John 14:26, what is one name for the Holy Spirit?
3. According to Hebrews 9:14, what in one fact about the Holy Spirit?
4. What was the name of the troublemaker who caused a revolt against Moses?
5. Who was the wicked man who murdered his brother, Abel?
6. Who was the wicked ruler of Judah who wanted to kill infant Jesus?
7. Who was the disciple who betrayed Jesus?
8. According to Proverbs 11:1, what is an abomination to God?
9. Who was the apostle to the Gentiles?
10. Who was the oldest man in the Bible?
11. Who was the short man who climbed a tree to see Jesus?
12. What book is mentioned in Malachi 3:16?
13. Who was Israel's first high priest?
14. Who led Israel out of bondage from Pharaoh and Egypt?
15. Who had the double anointing of Elijah?
16. Who was swallowed by a great fish because he was disobedient to God?
17. Where were believers first called "Christians?"
18. What was the birthplace of Jesus?
19. According to Matthew 5:16, what are believers to do?
20. When we are tempted, what are we to do?

21. According to James 5:13, what are the afflicted to do?
22. According to Ephesians 6:2, what are we to do for our father and mother?
23. What kind of wood did God tell Noah to use?
24. Who was the world's first couple?
25. On earth, who was the legal father of Jesus?
26. Who was the couple that died for lying to the apostles?
27. Who was Abraham's wife?
28. The very first curse was pronounced upon what creature?
29. According to Acts 6:8, what was Stephen full of?
30. Who gave the world's very first excuse?
31. Who was the prophetess present at Jesus' dedication?
32. What was the name of the river where Jesus was baptized?
33. What did Moses strike to get water?
34. According to Psalm 51:12, what is one thing we lose when we sin?
35. According to 2 Timothy 2:3, what are believers supposed to be?
36. Who was the Philistine woman that betrayed Samson?
37. As believers, what seasoning are we compared to in the earth?
38. Who was the young boy who would not partake of the king's meat and wine?
39. Who lost everything he had but was given back twice as much from the Lord?

Exercise Ten:

BIBLE SCRAMBLE

See who can unscramble these Bible names in the shortest amount of time. You can make your own Bible Scramble games, using categories that include the names of cities, animals or certain events pertaining to Bible characters. In addition, you may wish to let the children find and scramble their own words and present them for everyone to enjoy.

SET 1 – NEW TESTAMENT

1. LUPA_____   5. USEJS_____   9. LIPHIP_____

2. ERPTE_____   6. MASEJ_____   10. PHOSEJ_____

3. HJNO_____   7. YOHTTIM_____   11. KEUL_____

4. ARMY_____   8. ALISS_____   12. WHATMTE_____

SET 2 – OLD TESTAMENT

1. HELAJI_____   5. MAAD_____   9. LASIHE_____

2. SOEMS_____   6. AIVDD _____   10. REAMHIJE_____

3. LEINAD_____   7. MOONLOS_____   11. LEEKIZE_____

4. SONMAS_____   8. LEAMS_____   12. BOCAJ_____

SET 3 – OLD TESTAMENT TOUGHIES

1. SACHZAARI_____

2. POSHAAHHTJE_____

3. ZZAAEEBNUCHDRN_____

4. ZEEKHIAH_____

5. BAAKUKHK _____

6. AZHUI _____

7. ROAMICED_____

8. CAIMHIA_____

9. MENNABJI_____

10.BEENUR_____

SET 4 – NEW TESTAMENT TOUGHIES

1. RAISLLCIP_____

2. STARCAHIRSU_____

3. HAPSAPRI_____

4. AAANNSI_____

5. MAAGLLEI _____

6. WARHOTLOMBE _____

7. COMEDINSU_____

8. SAZECUHC_____

9. SIJAUR_____

10.RELSUNIOC _____

Exercise Eleven:

BIBLE DETECTIVE

Find out what doesn't fit in these Bible stories. Once you have fig-ured out the answers, have your children make up their own Bible myster-ies for a fun way to learn the Word of God. You can go to any length or any depth, mixing things up by using characters, quotes or places depend-ing on the ages of your children.

Story #1

King Saul had gathered his army to fight against the Philistines. The Israelites camped on one side of the hill, and the Philistines were camped on the other side. A mighty Philistine hero named Goliath came out of his camp, shouting to the Israelites, "If one of your men can kill me, we will be your slaves." All the Israelites were afraid of him and ran away. David had come to the hillside to bring his brothers some food. "Why are you afraid of Goliath? We belong to God. Nothing that stands against Him can stand against us." With that statement, David took his sling shot and went out to meet Goliath. David was surprised at how short Goliath was. He placed small stones in his sling, whirled it around over his head. One smooth stone hit Goliath in the head, and he fell dead.

Something is wrong here. Can you be a good Bible Detective and crack this case? What part of the story is not Biblical? _____

_____

Story #2

On the way to Rome, Paul's boat became shipwrecked. Fortunately, they were able to escape to the small island of Malta. The people were very friendly. Since it was still raining and very cold they built a fire so the shipwrecked passengers could keep warm. Paul also helped to gather sticks. After the fire had started, the heat of it attracted a bear from the jungle. Paul was bitten by the bear; but he just pushed him away. Everyone was amazed. They thought Paul would surely die from the bite, but he didn't. God was with him and instantly healed him.

Something is wrong here. Can you be a good Bible Detective and crack this case? What part of the story is not Biblical? _____

_____

Story #3

After Noah had obeyed God and built the ark, the entire earth was flooded by the rain. For 40 days the flood waters covered the earth. The waters had risen until everything living thing on the earth was destroyed. Even the birds of the air died because they had no place to go. Finally, God sent a wind and the waters began to go down. After many days, Noah knew that there was dry land because a dove he had sent out never returned to the ark. God made a promise to Noah after that. As a sign of His promise that the entire earth would never again be destroyed by a flood, God set the sun in the sky. Seeing the sun is a reminder of the covenant that God has with the people of the earth. When we see the sun, we can remember that God will never again destroy the world by a flood. He is true to His Word.

Something is wrong here. Can you be a good Bible Detective and crack this case? What part of the story is not Biblical? _____

_____

Exercise Twelve:

BIBLE GENIUS

It's time to see how smart you are with Bible facts and figures! After completing this exercise with your children, make up your own questions using the Bible. You may prepare them according to the level of difficulty or host a Bible Olympics with bronze, silver and gold medal questions.

1. When Jesus comes back in the Second Coming, what will He be riding?

   (a) A donkey   (b) A white horse   (c) A black horse   (d) A dove

2. When Paul and Silas were singing praises to God and an angel helped them to escape, where were they?

   (a) In a dungeon   (b) In a cave
   (c) In a ship   (d) In a tent

3. How did John the Baptist die?

   (a) He was crucified   (b) He was burned at the stake
   (c) He was beheaded   (d) He was sick

4. How many spies did Joshua send to Jericho?
   (a) 2   (b) 12   (c) 7   (d) 3

5. Which king prayed to live, and God answered him by adding 15 years to his life?
   (a) King David   (b) King Hezekiah
   (c) King Solomon   (d) King Saul

6. Where did God put Moses before showing him His glory?

   (a) On a ship   (b) In a house
   (c) In a deep hole   (d) In the cleft of a rock

7. To whom was Joseph was first sold?

   (a) The Amalekites   (b) The Hittites
   (c) The Ishmaelites   (d) The Egyptians

8. What prophet renounced David for his sin with Bathsheba?

   (a) Nathan   (b) Samuel
   (c) Micah   (d) Jeremiah

Exercise Thirteen:

LIFETIME CONFESSIONS

And thou shalt love the Lord thy God with all thine heart, and with all thy soul, and with all thy might. And these words...shall be in thine heart: And thou shalt teach them diligently unto thy children, and shalt talk of them when thou sittest in thine house, and when thou walkest by the way, and when thou liest down, and when thou risest up (Deuteronomy 6:5-7).

Confessions for women, men, husbands, wives, parents, children and teens were listed at the end of chapter 27, *Built on a Rock.* Those are only a few of the areas in which many people want to excel and experience God's power, abundance and goodness.

Take a moment to think about your life. What are some other areas in which you would like to prosper or see a breakthrough? The next four exercises provide you with an opportunity to write down specific confessions regarding your job, continued health and/or rapid healing and financial prosperity. The fourth confession page is blank, allowing you to write confessions for any other area in which you need to experience God's power. If there are several areas you want to make confessions over, copy and fill out the blank page accordingly.

Begin these exercises by searching for scriptures that support what you want to see happen in your life. Personalize the scriptures by using "I" or "Me." Place the scripture reference at the end of each statement. When you are finished, place these pages where you can see them every day, confess the Word of God over your life and experience success.

CONFESSIONS FOR MY JOB

Today's Date:_____

_____

_____

_____

_____

_____

_____

_____

_____

_____

_____

_____

_____

_____

_____

_____

_____

_____

_____

CONFESSIONS FOR GOOD HEALTH / RAPID HEALING

Today's Date:_____

_____

_____

_____

_____

_____

_____

_____

_____

_____

_____

_____

_____

_____

_____

_____

_____

_____

_____

CONFESSIONS FOR FINANCIAL PROSPERITY

Today's Date:_____

_____

_____

_____

_____

_____

_____

_____

_____

_____

_____

_____

_____

_____

_____

_____

_____

_____

_____

CONFESSIONS FOR _____

Today's Date:_____

_____

_____

_____

_____

_____

_____

_____

_____

_____

_____

_____

_____

_____

_____

_____

_____

_____

Exercise Fourteen:

ILLUSTRATIVE DEVOTIONALS

Often the best devotionals have illustrations that accompany them. The following devotionals involve a practical, "hands-on" approach. After you have exhausted these ideas, create other devotionals to present to your family.

Before you begin, read each account, find its focal point and create "hands-on" assignments to drive the point home. Be sure to keep your children's ages in mind. Children between the ages of five and seven have a 10-minute attention span. Eight to 12-year-olds have a 15-minute attention span. Remember, creativity is the key. Try not to preach to your children. Involve them in the story by activating their senses: sight, hearing, smell, taste and touch.

NAME THAT ANIMAL!
The Story of Creation
Genesis 1 and 2

Take the family outside for this Bible devotional. Make sure you have thoroughly meditated on each verse so as not to break the concentration of the lesson. As you begin to review the creation story in Genesis 1, point to the sky, clouds and sun. When talking about land, have family members hold dirt in their hands and examine it. Encourage the children to touch the trees, shrubs and grass. Find a flower, seedling or fruit to open and examine the seeds. Explain how these were all created differently from man-made items. According to God's plan, the seeds were placed inside the plants so they could reproduce themselves.

Water is another source that is given by God. Have some nearby so the children can examine it and allow it to run through their fingers. Comment that it would have been impossible for a human being to create it. Explain to them that natural things have their point of origin in God. Now point to the birds and insects and explain that God created them to reproduce after their own kind. Note the colors of the feathers, scales or skin and how each one varies. Mention other animals and how God created them as well.

Next, discuss with the children that God made human beings in His own image (Genesis 2). Talk about your bodies and how they have been wonderfully made. Explain to the children that God didn't have a name for all the animals and birds He created, so He allowed man (Adam) to name them. Just for fun, ask them to name the plants and animals they see.

ROCK ANIMALS

For this devotional, you will need rocks and paint, and if desired, other fun decorations such as plastic eyes, eyelashes, feathers, yarn or beads. Don't forget to include glue!

When the children have finally run out of names, it's time for a "hands-on" project. Take a walk to examine rocks, in all shapes and forms. Remember to point out that God created those rocks. Pick one up and say what animal that rock looks like. Look for odd shapes that might resemble an elephant's trunk, or a rabbit with ears, or a dog or cat curled up for a lazy nap. When everyone has found a "rock animal," take them inside to paint the rocks and transform them into the "animals" they saw. Once the children have created their "rock animals," they can give them special names, just like Adam did. Now they have their very own pet rocks, complete with the memory of God's creation!

PLAYING "HEARTS"
The Parable of the Sower
Mark 4:3-9

Read aloud to your children the story of the farmer (sower) who went to sow seed in his field. Examine the conditions of the soil in which the farmer planted his seed and compare it to the condition of people's hearts. Explain that Jesus was comparing a farmer planting seed in a field to a person planting the seed of God's message in his or her heart. Just as there are different soil conditions, people have different "heart" conditions. How did Jesus bring these points out?

1. Seed was scattered on the wayside.

These types of people hear the gospel message, but allow Satan to take it out of their hearts. The term "wayside" is used because they either forgot the Word or didn't pay any attention to what they heard. A person can "hear" and not "listen." Explain to your children that listening means receiving and understanding what is said. (Note: You may use an example of a radio playing when they are with their friends. They "hear" the radio playing, but their attention is focused on their friends. Therefore, they "hear" the radio but aren't "listening" to it.) Be sure to ask the following questions: "Have you known of people who just weren't interested in God? Could it be because they never took the time to know Him? Is it important to know Him as your best friend and as your heavenly Father? Is it important to know His ways and how He speaks? How will you take the time to continue knowing Him?"

2. Some seed fell on stony ground that did not have much earth.

These people receive the Word and are excited about it, but when trouble comes, they forget what the Word has to say about their situation. Ultimately, they fall away from God. Why? Their hearts become hardened because they neglect to "feed" themselves from the Word of God; there-fore, they don't have any roots. Ask the children to think of how it would be to plant a flower on top of a rock. What would happen? The flower would die because there would be no place for its roots to go. The same is true when we don't keep the Word in our hearts and allow it to mature us spiritually. Unless we read the Bible daily and allow its principles to take root in our lives, we will die spiritually. Ask your children the following questions "Can you remember a time when you were mad about something and refused to hear the truth?" Encourage discussion, then say, "That's how a stony heart rejects the truth. We must keep our hearts soft at all costs."

3.   Other seed fell among thorns.

These people hear the message of God but often give in to worry and quickly forget the truth. Their priorities are skewed, so thorns and weeds take root in their hearts and choke God's Word. As a result, they are unable to follow Him wholeheartedly. These people don't produce any fruit in their lives. Sometimes it's even hard to tell if they are Christians because of their actions or lifestyles. Ask your children the following ques-tions: "Can you remember a time when you worried about something and someone had to remind you of what the Word of God said before you felt better?" "What if you were never reminded of the Word? How would you have continued to feel? Would those worries climb up like thorns and make you upset? Would your thoughts be consumed by the worries?" That's

52

how the thorns choke out the Word of God from people's lives.

4.   Some seed was scattered on good soil.

These individuals have prepared their hearts to listen to the Word and act on what they've heard. By putting biblical principles into action, they keep the soil of their hearts fertile, or ready to receive more "nutrients" from the Word of God. Because of this, they continue to grow and produce the fruit of the Spirit (Galatians 5:22-23). Their lifestyles are pleasing to God and often lead others to Jesus. Ask your children the following questions: "What are some ways that you can keep your heart soft to the ways of the Lord?" "What will that action produce in your life?"

EARTH PALS

For this devotional project you will need:

1 pair of pantyhose (use different colors to make different "races")

Potting soil (about 1/2 cup per earth pal)

Rye grass seed

Rubber bands

Glue

Plastic eyes or buttons

Red, peach or cream felt (for cheeks and mouths)

Pipe cleaners (for glasses)

Put one of your hands into the first leg of the pantyhose and push straight to the end until taut. Then pull the second pantyhose leg over your hand. You now have both legs of the pantyhose together as one leg.

- Pour in a handful of rye grass seed, making sure it goes all the way to the toe.

- Pour in your potting soil.

- Twist the hose tightly and tie off with a rubber band. Cut off all excess hosiery.

- Pull out a small pinch on each side of the "ball" and rubber band it off to make ears. Pinch out a small section in the front for the nose and rubber band it off.

- Decorate with eyes, a felt mouth, pipe cleaner glasses and so on.

- Place your earth pal in a plastic butter dish in one inch of water. Set in a sunny spot, preferably by a window.

In about four days, you'll have green "hair" sprouting from the top of your earth pal's head. Keep him watered and sitting in a sunny window. It's a fun new buddy for your child—and a wonderful reminder of the amount of time it took God to create man as well as what sowing seed in good soil can produce!

Exercise Fifteen:

SCRIPTURE MEMORIZATION GAMES

To aid in Scripture memorization, try the following exercise. Cut a piece of poster board, construction paper or typing paper into several strips. Select a Bible verse and write one word on each strip. You can either hang the strips on the wall or refrigerator, or place the pieces on a table. If your child is not yet able to read, use pictures in place of the words whenever possible. Say the verse aloud together, then do one or more of the following:

- **Missing in Action:** Remove a strip and say the verse aloud. Continue until all the strips are gone and you can recite the verse from memory.

- **Bible Scramble:** Say the verse aloud together several times, then put the strips face down on the floor. Tell the children that you are going to time them on how long it takes them to unscramble the pieces. The child who does it the fastest wins a treat. Continue until every child has won.

- **Bible Pass:** Pass a Bible around the group while music is playing. Whoever is left holding the Bible when the music stops has to say the memory verse.

- **Musical Chairs:** Whoever is left standing will be allowed to remain in the game if he or she can quote the memory verse correctly.

Exercise Sixteen:

DEVELOPING ORIGINAL OBJECT LESSONS

1. Keep an idea file. Whenever an idea pops into your mind, write it down and file it. Don't be concerned about the details. They will come later.

2. Looking through magazines, children's books and novelty catalogs will often spark creativity. Don't leave out schoolbooks, either. In addition, television sitcoms can often give you a topic to discuss with your teenagers.

3. Waiting on the Lord and allowing Him to speak to you is the most effective way to get ideas. He knows what each member of your family needs, and He will tell you.

4. As you read the Bible daily, look for opportunities to illustrate a point visually. The Bible is loaded with ideas!

5. Make the object lesson entertaining, colorful and simple.

6. Visit a bookstore or library and purchase or check out devotionals or activity books you can use at home.

7. Ask for help! Don't be afraid to ask your pastor, child's Sunday school teacher or other parents for object lesson ideas.

ANSWER KEY

Exercise One: The Transformation Process

1) Spirit, soul and body
2) Are, possess, live in
3) Dust, spirit
4) Heaven
5) Hell
6) Mind, will, emotions
7) Spirit, soul
8) Dead
9) Sin
10) Reborn, new life, born again
11) Spirit, soul, body
12) Renew, transform, mind, thoughts agree
13) Mind, will, emotions, actions, desires, spirit

Exercise Five: Bible Jeopardy

Possible answers:

1. Psalm 118:17; 103:3; Jeremiah 17:14; 30:17; Matthew 9:35; Luke 6:19; Hebrews 13:8

2. Psalm 91:1-7, 10-11; Isaiah 54:14; Psalm 56:11; Proverbs 3:25-26; Psalm 112:7

3. Psalm 91:11; 121:2-3; 3:5-6; 4:8; 62:5, 6; 23:1-4

4. Romans 8:35, 37; Matthew 28:20; Psalm 3:3; Isaiah 54:4-5

5. Psalm 23:4; 56:3; 27:1; Isaiah 65:24; 41:10; Psalm 138:7; Luke 10:19; Joshua 1:9; Proverbs 3:25-26; 1 John 5:4; Psalm 91

6. Philippians 1:6; 2:13; 2 Chronicles 20:15; Hebrews 12:2; 13:5; Matthew 28:20; Romans 8:31; Psalm 91:2; Galatians 6:9; Isaiah 41:10

Exercise Six: Salvation Basics

1) T   2) T   3) F   4) T   5) T   6) T   7) F

Exercise Seven: Time Out for Families

1) Jeroboam (1 Kings 12:25)
2) Ben (1 Chronicles 15:18)
3) harps (2 Samuel 6:5)
4) Silas (Acts 15:40)
5) Gamaliel (Acts 22:3)
6) Moses (Exodus 2:5-10)
7) David (Acts 13:22)
8) Paul (Acts 9:3-9; 13:9)
9) Esther (Esther 4:14)
10) Joppa (Acts 9:36)
11) Gad (Genesis 30;10-11)
12) Joseph (Genesis 37:4-9)
13) Luke (Colossians 3:14;
    2 Timothy 4:11; Philemon 24)

14) Isaiah (2 Kings 20:1)
15) Amos (Amos 3:3)
16) net (Mark 1:16)
17) vase
18) Jehoshaphat40)
    (2 Chronicles 20:18-19)
19) Daniel (Daniel 6:16)
20) Perez (Genesis 38:27-29)
21) Barak (Judges 4:4-8)

22) Elijah (2 Kings 2:11)
23) Obadiah (Obadiah 1-21)
24) Aquila (Acts 18:2)
25) Bathsheba (Matthew 1:6)
26) Ham (Genesis 5:32)
27) Philip (Acts 8:39)
28) Peter (Mark 14:66-72)
29) gourd (Jonah 4:6)
20) Lazarus (John 11:43-44)
31) Malachi
32) prison (Acts 16:26)
33) Jude
34) Boaz (Ruth 4:13)
35) Josiah (2 Chronicles 34:1;
    Matthew 1:11)
36) Uriah (2 Samuel 11:2-3)
37) Caleb (Numbers 13:26-30)
38) Eve (Genesis 3:20)
39) tale (Exodus 5:8)
40) Mark (Acts 15:39; 2
    Timothy 4:11)
41) Huz (Genesis 22:21)
42) Asa (1 Kings 15:23)

Exercise Eight: Joseph's Secret Egyptian Code

The correct number is 29.

Exercise Nine: Bible Trivia

1) Jonathan (1 Samual 18:1)
2) The Comforter
3) He is eternal
4) Korah (Numbers 16)
5) Cain (Genesis 4:8)
6) Herod the Great (Matthew 2)
7) Judas Iscariot (John 12:6)

8) A false balance
9) Paul (Romans 11:13)
10) Methuselah (Genesis 5:27)
11) Zacchaeus (Luke 19:3-4)
12) Book of Remembrance
13) Aaron (Leviticus 8:2)
14) Moses (Exodus 3:1-12)
15) Elisha (2 Kings 1:1-13)
16) Jonah (Jonah 1:1-2)
17) Antioch (Acts 11:26)
18) Bethlehem (Luke 2:4-7)
19) Let their light shine

20) Count it all joy (James 1:2)
21) Pray
22) Honor them
23) Gopher wood (Genesis 6:14)
24) Adam and Eve (Gen. 3:20)
25) Joseph (Luke 1:27)
26) Ananias and Sapphira (Acts 5:1)
27) Sarah (Genesis 18:9)
28) Serpent (Genesis 3:14)
29) Faith and power
30) Adam (Genesis 3:12)
31) Anna (Luke 2:36)
32) Jordan (Matthew 3:13)
33) A rock (Exodus 17:6)
34) Joy
35) Good soldiers
36) Delilah (Judges 16)
37) Salt (Matthew 5:13)
38) Daniel (Daniel 1:8)

Exercise Ten: Bible Scramble

Set 1: Paul, Peter, John, Mary, Jesus, James, Timothy, Silas, Philip, Joseph, Luke, Matthew

Set 2: Elijah, Moses, Daniel, Samson, Adam, David, Solomon, Samuel, Elisha, Jeremiah, Ezekiel, Jacob

Set 3: Zacharias, Jehoshaphat, Nebuchadnezzar, Hezekiah, Habakkuk, Uzziah, Mordecai, Micaiah, Benjamin, Reuben

Set 4: Priscilla, Aristarchus, Sapphira, Ananias, Gamaliel, Bartholomew, Nicodemus, Zaccheus, Jairus, Cornelius

Exercise Eleven: Bible Detective

Story #1

Goliath *wasn't* short; in fact, he was more than 9 feet tall! But Goliath's height didn't bother David at all. He was secure in God and had great faith. Read 1 Samuel 17 for the correct story.

Story #2

It wasn't a bear that attacked Paul; a poisonous snake jumped out of the fire and bit him. He wasn't hurt, though; he just shook it off as a testimony to the power of God. Read Acts 27 & 28 for the correct story.

Story #3

It *wasn't* the sun! God set a rainbow in the sky to mark His covenant with humanity. Every time we see a beautiful rainbow, we can rest assured that a flood will never again destroy the earth. Read Genesis 8 and 9 for the correct story.

Exercise Twelve: Bible Genius

1) White horse (Revelation 19:11)
2) A dungeon (Acts 16:24-26)
3) Beheaded (Matthew 14:10)
4) 2 (Joshua 2:10)
5) King Hezekiah (2 Kings 20:1-6)
6) In the cleft of a rock (Exodus 33:22)
7) The Ishmaelites (Genesis 37:28)
8) Nathan (2 Samuel 12)

NOTES

NOTES

NOTES

NOTES